Morning to Midnight Cook Book

340 Unexpected Treats from
Aunt Jemima

Photographs by *George Ratkai/Paul Dome*

Illustrations by *Joan Blume*

FOLLETT PUBLISHING COMPANY
CHICAGO • NEW YORK

There's a new kind of cooking and baking

. . . going on in your kitchen—and in ours—producing delicious, more varied, more exciting meals, in new and easy ways. From breakfast through lunches, dinners, meals-on-the-go, and meals-in-between, we enjoy a new range of eating adventure. Specialties from around the world—and treats which once were limited to "baking day" in the homes of good cooks—are everyday fare now. Any hour is mealtime. We still enjoy the best of the old, of course, and the very best recipes are here— for the day you want to bake a fine bread, or turn out a batch of old fashioned cookies. Here are easy shortcuts, too, using prepared mixes in unexpected ways for modern favorites, and menus to help you plan meals your family and friends will enjoy.

On cover: Counterclockwise, Corn Meal Yeast Rolls, p. 90; Apple Cinnamon Coffee Cake, p. 97; Cocktail Kabobs, p. 8; Cherry Crepes Supreme, p. 116; Cheese Puff Tower, p. 9. Center, for a regal meal, Crown Roast of Pork with Corn Bread Stuffing, p. 66.

CONTENTS

Morning to Midnight Cook Book contains menu suggestions for all important meal-time situations—with the exception of our Appetizers and Snacks chapter and our Breads and Desserts chapter. Following each menu are many of the recipes called for. These are marked with a single asterisk (*). In some instances, you will find a recipe listed in a menu which appears elsewhere in the book. These are indicated by double asterisks (**), and a footnote will direct you to another page for that recipe. All recipes which are illustrated in the book carry a cross-reference line directly under the recipe title. It will point the way to the correct four-color photograph.

CHAPTER I

Appetizers and Snacks

The little meals between meals open the door to a new kind of food enjoyment—hospitality on tap for family and friends to suit any hour of the day, or any mood. It may be only a nibble, bite-size appetizers to serve with beverages, or it may be a repast substantial enough for that any-time-of-the-day Fourth Meal which has become so much a part of our American way of eating.

Be prepared with unusual ways to use handy mixes to short-cut preparation, and keep your larder supplied with ready-to-heat foods, which lend themselves to new menu tricks.

CHERRY DELIGHT COFFEE CAKE

1 package Aunt Jemima Coffee Cake Easy Mix	½ cup milk
1 egg	½ cup canned cherry pie filling

Preheat the oven to 375° F. Remove bag of coffee cake mix from package, add egg and milk, prepare according to package directions. When completely blended, squeeze *half* the batter into the foil pan included in the package. Spoon the cherry pie filling over this batter, cover with remaining batter. Sprinkle with topping mix contained in smaller bag, spreading evenly. Bake about 25 minutes or until topping is golden. *Makes 8 servings.*

BUTTER CRUNCH COFFEE CAKE

Topping:	*Cake:*
½ cup butter or margarine, melted	2 eggs
½ cup granulated sugar	¾ cup granulated sugar
½ cup pecan halves	¾ cup milk
	2 cups Aunt Jemima Buttermilk Pancake Mix
	5 tablespoons butter or margarine, melted

Preheat oven to 350° F. Combine melted butter and sugar for topping, spread over bottom of 11 x 7 x 2-inch baking pan. Arrange pecan halves over bottom of pan. In mixing bowl, beat eggs and sugar until fluffy; stir in milk, then pancake mix and melted butter; blend until dry ingredients are thoroughly moistened. Pour cake batter over topping. Bake about 30 to 35 minutes until a cake-tester inserted in center comes out clean. Cool in pan 5 minutes; turn out upside down. Cut. Serve warm. *Makes 10–12 servings.*

CHEE-CHEE CORN MUFFINS

1 package (12 oz.) Flako Corn Muffin Mix	⅔ cup milk
1 egg	1 cup grated sharp cheese
	¼ teaspoon oregano

Preheat oven to 400° F. Grease 14 medium muffin cups. Combine corn muffin mix, egg, milk, cheese and oregano, stir just until dry ingredients are thoroughly moistened. Spoon into muffin cups, filling half full. Bake about 15 minutes until golden. *Makes 14 medium-sized muffins.*

SPICY FRUIT CUP CAKES

1 package Flako Cup Cake Mix	1 cup unpeeled chopped red apples; or ½ cup raisins; or ½ cup chopped canned peaches, well-drained
1 egg	
½ cup milk	
½ teaspoon cinnamon	
¼ teaspoon allspice	

Preheat oven to 350° F. Grease 12 large muffin cups. Combine cup cake mix, egg, milk, spices and fruit; blend just until dry ingredients are thoroughly moistened. Spoon batter into muffin cups, filling half full. Bake about 20 to 25 minutes until golden. Delicious hot from the oven or cool. *Makes 12 large cup cakes.*

MEATY STICKS

Heat frozen Aunt Jemima Corn Sticks. Make sandwiches with folded slices of luncheon meat between two corn sticks. Great for after-school appetites, and something the youngsters can put together quickly.

CALICO POPCORN BRITTLE

5 cups popped popcorn	2 tablespoons vinegar
½ cup salted peanuts	1 tablespoon butter or margarine
1 cup Aunt Jemima Syrup	

Place popcorn and peanuts in a large bowl. Combine syrup and vinegar in a deep saucepan, boil until mixture reaches the soft crack stage (290° F. on a candy thermometer), or until a small amount of syrup dropped in cold water separates into small threads. Remove from heat; add butter. Promptly pour syrup over popcorn and peanuts, mixing quickly until coated. Spread on buttered baking sheet; cool thoroughly. Break into pieces. *Makes about 5 cups.*

LEMON-GLAZED DOUGHNUTS

3½ cups Aunt Jemima Pancake Mix	Oil for deep fat frying (about 2 cups)
⅔ cup granulated sugar	1 tablespoon lemon juice
1 teaspoon cinnamon	¾ cup sifted confectioners sugar
2 eggs	
¾ cup milk	
2 tablespoons melted butter or margarine	

Combine pancake mix, sugar and cinnamon, stir to blend well. Beat together eggs, milk, and butter, stir into pancake mix mixture, beat just until smooth. Drop dough by teaspoons into hot deep fat heated to 375° F. Cook about 2 to 3 minutes until golden, turning once. Remove with slotted spoon; drain on absorbent paper. Allow to cool. Blend lemon juice into confectioners sugar to form glaze; dribble glaze over cooled doughnuts. *Makes about 2½ dozen doughnuts.*

BOOSTER BARS

¼ cup sifted all-purpose flour	¾ cup firmly-packed light brown sugar
¾ teaspoon baking powder	½ cup raisins
1½ teaspoons salt	½ cup semi-sweet chocolate pieces
1 cup Quaker Oats (quick or old fashioned, uncooked)	½ cup butter or margarine, melted
4 cups instant nonfat dry milk	1 egg, beaten
	½ cup water

Preheat oven to 350° F. Grease a baking pan 11 x 7 x 2 inches. Sift together flour, baking powder and salt. Combine in a large bowl with oats, nonfat dry milk, brown sugar, raisins and chocolate pieces. Allow melted butter to cool, then add egg and water; stir this into oats mixture, blending well. Spread batter evenly over bottom of greased baking pan. Bake about 25 to 30 minutes until golden. Cool in pan about 10 minutes. Cut. *Makes 12 bars.*

TOASTER TARTS

1 package Flako Pie Crust Mix	Fruit preserves (blackberry, strawberry, or blueberry jam)
1 tablespoon sugar	
1 egg, beaten	

Empty pie crust mix in bowl. Add sugar and egg, stir with fork until mixture is dampened throughout. (If too dry, add a teaspoon of cold water.) Form into a ball; divide dough in half. Roll out each half between waxed paper into 8 x 12-inch rectangle. Cut into three 4 x 8-inch pieces. Repeat with remaining dough. Place about 2 teaspoons of preserves on each rectangle, moisten edges, and fold over to form a square, pressing edges with fork to seal. Prick pastry with fork. Bake in oven preheated to 400° F. about 10 minutes. Cool. Wrap in plastic bags and freeze until needed. To reheat, pop in toaster. *Makes 6 tarts.*

CHOCOLATE PASTRIES

Prepare pastry as for the Toaster Tarts. Roll out to form 2 squares, 12 inches each, cut these into 12 strips, each 2 x 6 inches. Place a section from a 9-oz. chocolate bar in each piece of pastry, moisten edges, fold over and seal. Bake in oven preheated to 400° F. about 15 minutes until crust is golden. *Makes 12 pastries.*

CHICKEN FRITTERS

1 teaspoon or envelope chicken stock concentrate	1 egg, beaten
1 teaspoon poultry seasoning	1 cup Aunt Jemima Pancake Mix
½ cup boiling water	1 cup diced cooked or canned chicken

Dissolve chicken stock concentrate and poultry seasoning in boiling water. Cool. Add to pancake mix with egg; blend well. Stir in chicken; let stand 5 minutes. Drop batter by teaspoons into hot deep fat heated to 375° F. Fry until nicely browned on each side, about 1 to 2 minutes. Drain on absorbent paper. Serve with Curry Mayonnaise or Sweet Mustard Dip (see below). *Makes about 25.*

Curry Mayonnaise. Blend 1 teaspoon curry powder with ½ cup mayonnaise.

Sweet Mustard Dip. Add 1 tablespoon prepared mustard and ¼ cup Aunt Jemima Syrup to ¼ cup melted butter or margarine. Serve hot.

BLINIS

Pancakes:	*Topping:*
1 egg	1 cup dairy sour cream
¾ cup milk	1 tablespoon minced raw onion
1 cup Aunt Jemima Buckwheat Pancake Mix	Black or red caviar; chopped hard-cooked egg; or chopped smoked fish filets
Butter or margarine, about 1 tablespoon	

Beat egg until foamy, add with milk to buckwheat pancake mix, stir until well blended. Let stand ½ hour. Melt a little of the butter in hot skillet heated to 400° F. Make pancakes 1½ to 2 inches in diameter, adding more butter to skillet if needed before each batch. Serve warm topped with a spoonful of dairy sour cream blended with minced onion, topping cream with caviar, chopped egg or smoked fish. (Blinis may be kept warm—wrapped in foil—in oven until time to serve.) *Makes about 20.*

PANCAKE CANAPÉS

Prepare Aunt Jemima Pancake Mix according to package directions. Drop by teaspoons onto hot, lightly greased skillet; pancakes should not be more than 1½ inches in diameter. Turn when tops are covered with bubbles and edges look cooked. Turn only once. Top with any of the following, to serve warm as party appetizers:

· Cream cheese blended with chopped olives

· Crumbled cooked bacon blended with cottage cheese

· Crumbled cooked bacon blended with chutney

· Deviled ham blended with a very little dairy sour cream

· Dairy sour cream and onion dip

SAUSAGES IN ORANGE BLANKETS

3 cans (4 oz. each)
Vienna sausages
¼ cup butter or margarine,
melted
1 cup Aunt Jemima
Buttermilk Pancake Mix

2 tablespoons orange juice
½ teaspoon grated orange
peel

Cut each sausage in half. In mixing bowl, combine butter and pancake mix, stir to blend. Sprinkle in orange juice and grated peel, toss with fork until lightly blended. Roll out between waxed paper to ⅛ inch thick. Cut into strips long enough to wrap around sausages. Wrap a strip of pastry around each sausage half, moistening edges to seal. Place on ungreased baking sheets, overlapped side down. Bake in oven preheated to 425° F. about 15 minutes until golden and crisp. *Makes about 42.*

BLINTZES

Filling:

1 egg
1 package (8 oz.) creamed
cottage cheese
2 packages (3 oz. each)
cream cheese, softened
½ teaspoon salt
1 tablespoon sugar
½ teaspoon grated
lemon peel

Pancakes:

2 eggs
1⅓ cups water
1 cup Aunt Jemima
Pancake Mix
Butter or margarine,
about 2 tablespoons

Dairy sour cream for
topping

To make filling: Beat egg until foamy. Beat in cottage cheese, cream cheese, salt, sugar and lemon peel, until smooth. Set aside.

To make pancakes: Beat eggs until frothy, add water and pancake mix, beat until smooth. Melt a small amount of the butter in small skillet (7 inch); add 1 tablespoon batter, tilting pan to coat evenly (as for crepes). Flip when browned on bottom, cook on the other side. Repeat with remaining batter.

Place a tablespoon of filling on each pancake, fold over sides, then roll. Place on serving platter, overlapped side down. Serve at once, topped with sour cream. (Or the filled blintzes may be frozen, to be reheated later in butter or margarine, served with sour cream.)

COCKTAIL KABOBS

Pictured on cover

¼ cup soy sauce
¼ cup medium dry sherry
¼ cup Aunt Jemima Syrup
⅛ teaspoon garlic powder
Pinch of ginger
24 canned pineapple
chunks, drained

1 banana, cut in 12 chunks
(optional)
1 lb. unsliced boiled ham,
cubed

Combine soy sauce, sherry, syrup, garlic powder and ginger in bowl. Marinate the pineapple and ham in sauce for several hours. Remove, drain, insert on each bamboo skewer 2 pineapple chunks (or use 2 pineapple chunks and 1 banana chunk) and 2 ham cubes. Broil 3 inches from heat, turning once, until lightly browned, about 2 to 3 minutes. *Makes 12 kabobs.*

STUFFED MUSHROOMS

24 large mushrooms
1 medium onion, minced
¼ cup butter or margarine,
melted
2 teaspoons minced parsley
2 tablespoons Parmesan
cheese

1 frozen Aunt Jemima
Corn Stick, or small
muffin, toasted, crumbled
¼ teaspoon seasoning salt

Stem mushrooms; chop stems and sauté with the minced onion in a little more than half the butter. Remove from heat, add parsley, cheese, the crumbled corn stick and seasoning salt. Use mixture to stuff mushroom caps. Brush remaining butter over mushroom caps, place on broiler rack and broil 4 inches from heat until lightly browned, about 5 minutes. *Makes 24.*

CHEESE PUFF TOWER

Pictured on cover.

¾ cup butter or margarine
1½ cups water
1 package Flako Popover Mix

6 eggs
2 pressurized cans (4¾ oz. each) cheese spread

Preheat oven to 400° F. Lightly grease baking sheet. Place butter and water in 2-quart saucepan, bring water to a boil over high heat, stir until butter melts. Reduce heat, add popover mix, beat vigorously until mixture leaves sides of pan in compact ball. Remove from heat, quickly add eggs one at a time, beating smooth after each addition. After all eggs are added, beat until mixture has satin sheen. Drop by heaping teaspoons on greased baking sheet, bake about 30 minutes or until golden. Cool on rack. To fill, press nozzle of pressurized can through side of each puff, press to force a small amount of cheese into puff.

To make tower: Cut a circle of foil 9 inches in diameter. For base, dab 7 puffs with cheese, place in ring on foil. For second row, use 5 puffs, securing with cheese spread, then continue building pyramid in decreasing circles, using cheese to fill crevices and hold puffs together. Refrigerate completed tower until time to serve.

BITE-SIZE QUICHE LORRAINE

2 packages Flako Pie Crust Mix, or pastry for two 2-crust pies
1 egg white, slightly beaten
6 oz. Swiss or Gruyere cheese, shredded

½ cup slivered cooked ham
4 eggs
½ teaspoon salt
¼ teaspoon nutmeg
⅛ teaspoon white pepper
1 pint heavy cream

Prepare pie crust mix according to package directions (or your favorite recipe), roll out to ⅛ inch

thick, cut into 4-inch rounds. Place each pastry round on a circle of heavy aluminum foil cut to the same size. Dip bottom of small bottle in flour, place floured bottle in center of dough, flute pastry and foil to form edging. Prick pastry with a fork. Brush bottom with egg white. Bake 5 minutes in oven preheated to 375° F. Remove from oven, sprinkle cheese and ham over bottom of each. Beat together eggs, seasoning and cream; divide mixture evenly over the cheese and ham in the pastry shells. Return to oven about 15 minutes or until a knife inserted in center of filling comes out clean. Serve warm. *Makes about 2 dozen.*

To freeze for future use: Prepare and fill pastry shells as above. Freeze until firm. Wrap and store. Allow 20 to 25 minutes to bake frozen Quiche.

CHEESE STRAWS

1 package Flako Pie Crust Mix
1 tablespoon caraway seed

Dash of salt and pepper
1 cup grated Cheddar cheese
¼ cup ice water

Empty contents of package of pie crust mix in a large mixing bowl. Add caraway seed, salt, pepper and grated cheese. Sprinkle in cold water, a tablespoon at a time, stirring with fork until dough holds together. Add an extra tablespoon of water, if necessary, to hold together. Form into a ball and chill about 15 minutes. Roll out to about ¼ inch thick on a lightly floured board. Cut into strips about 4 inches long and ½ inch wide. Twist each strip once in center and place on an ungreased baking sheet. Bake in oven preheated to 400° F. until a light golden brown, about 12 minutes. Serve hot or cold. Cheese twists may be frozen or stored in a tightly covered canister for a week or more. *Makes 2½ dozen.*

ASPARAGUS FINGERS

1 package frozen Aunt Jemima Corn Sticks	1 can (1 lb.) green asparagus spears, drained
Whipped or softened butter or margarine	Pimiento strips

Place frozen corn sticks on ungreased baking sheet flat side up. Spread each with very small amount of softened butter. Place 2 asparagus spears on each corn stick, lay a strip of pimiento across each. (This can be done ahead.) Just before serving, place in oven preheated to 450° F. about 5 minutes. Serve warm. *Makes 12 fingers.*

CHEESY CORN STICKS

Spread flat side of frozen corn sticks with processed cheese spread, or place a strip of American cheese (cut to fit) over each corn stick. Place under broiler just until cheese melts; serve hot.

WAFFLE APPETITE TEASERS

Heat frozen Aunt Jemima Country Waffles or prepare waffles with Aunt Jemima Pancake Mix according to package direction. Cut hot waffles into small circles, triangles and squares. Top some with cheese mixture, others with ham mixture.

CHEESE

2 egg whites	½ cup grated sharp cheese
½ teaspoon paprika	Sliced stuffed olives

Beat egg whites until stiff. Fold in paprika and cheese. Place small mound of cheese mixture on half the waffle "canapés." Bake in oven preheated to 350° F. about 5 to 7 minutes. Serve each topped with an olive slice. *Makes 15 canapés.*

HAM

1 cup ground cooked ham	2 tablespoons sweet pickle relish
2 tablespoons mayonnaise	Parsley sprigs
1 tablespoon prepared mustard	

Combine ham, mayonnaise, mustard and pickle relish, blending well. Spread on waffle bases; top with sprigs of parsley. *Makes 15 canapés.*

PIROSHKI

½ lb. ground beef (raw or cooked)	1 tablespoon minced dill weed or parsley
2 tablespoons butter or margarine	½ cup cooked rice, or 2 hard-cooked eggs, minced
2 tablespoons chopped onion	1 package Flako Pie Crust Mix, or recipe for 2-crust pie
½ teaspoon salt	
2 tablespoons dairy sour cream	

Sauté beef in butter until it loses its color; add onion, cook, stirring, until onion is soft. Add salt, sour cream, dill weed or parsley and rice or chopped eggs; mix well. Prepare pie crust according to package directions (or your favorite recipe); roll out to ⅛ inch thick. Cut into 2-inch rounds. In the center of each round, place a heaping teaspoon of the meat mixture. Moisten edges of pastry, fold over, press edges together. Bake piroshki on ungreased baking sheets in oven preheated to 425° F. until crisply golden, about 25 minutes. *Makes about 25.*

HOT ANCHOVY WAFFLE STICKS

Toast frozen Aunt Jemima Country Waffles as directed on package. While still warm spread with anchovy butter; cut each waffle into 4 "sticks." Serve hot.

EMPANADITAS

1 package Flako Pie Crust Mix, or recipe for 2-crust pie	¼ cup spicy-hot barbecue sauce
1½ cups chopped cooked meat (beef or lamb) or fish	1 green chili pepper, chopped (optional)

Prepare pie crust mix according to package directions (or your favorite recipe); roll out to ⅛ inch thick. Cut into 2-inch rounds. Heat together the chopped meat (or fish) and barbecue sauce; add the chopped chili pepper. Place a heaping teaspoon of meat mixture in each pastry round; moisten edges, fold over rounds, and press edges with tines of fork, pricking top of pastry. Place on ungreased baking sheet. Bake in oven preheated to 425° F., until golden, about 20 minutes. *Makes about 25.*

Cheese Empanaditas. Instead of meat or fish and barbecue sauce, place a small chunk of cheese, such as Monterey Jack or mild Cheddar, and a dab of dairy sour cream in each pastry round; fold over and seal edges, then bake as above.

PASTRY PINWHEELS

1 package Flako Pie Crust Mix	1 teaspoon caraway seed or red pepper flakes
6 tablespoons dairy sour cream	1 can (4 oz.) liver paté
4 oz. Cheddar cheese, grated	

Prepare pie crust mix as directed on package, but use sour cream in place of water. Roll out half the dough on a floured surface to ⅛ inch thick, forming a rectangle 8 x 10 inches. Sprinkle dough with cheese, caraway seed, or pepper flakes. Starting with long side, roll up like jelly roll, moisten edges of pastry and seal. Place edge down in foil, plastic wrap or waxed paper, and wrap. Chill 15 minutes. Cut into slices ½ inch thick. Place on ungreased baking sheet cut side down. Bake in oven preheated to 425° F. about 10 to 12 minutes.

Roll out remaining dough, spread with liver paté, and roll up, slice and bake in same way. *Makes 40.*

DIP-A-RAMA

Toast frozen Aunt Jemima Corn Sticks, cut each in half. Serve hot with a selection of savory dips, such as:

AVOCADO DIP

1 envelope dehydrated onion soup mix	2 cups mashed avocado
	Few drops lemon juice

Blend soup mix with avocado; sprinkle with lemon juice. *Makes 2¼ cups.*

CHILI DIP

1 can (1 lb.) chili	1 tablespoon Worcestershire sauce
¼ cup chili sauce	

Combine ingredients, beat in blender until smooth. *Makes about 2 cups.*

EASY RAREBIT DIP

1 can (10¾ oz.) condensed Cheddar cheese soup	1 tablespoon Worcestershire sauce
⅓ cup milk	1 teaspoon prepared mustard

Combine ingredients in saucepan, bring just to a boil. Serve hot as a dip. (Or, for a midnight snack, serve this same mixture *over* toasted corn sticks.)

CHAPTER II

Breakfasts and Brunches
for all seasons

Welcome the day with a bright start—a breakfast that is your personal "clear day" forecast. Whether it's a meal in jig-time, a leisurely Sunday breakfast with the family, or a very special company brunch, plan the menu to match the season. Add warmth to a winter day, or cool calm to a summer morning for every member of the family.

Some enjoy the same foods for breakfast every morning; others look for adventures in taste. Whatever your breakfast pattern, be sure to make it well-balanced and packed with nutrition, for breakfast is in many ways the most important meal of the day.

WINTER MORN

GRAPEFRUIT WITH MAPLE-FLAVORED SYRUP

*CORNED BEEF HASH NESTS WITH EGGS

*COLONEL CORN MUFFINS

*FRUITED COFFEE CAKE

COFFEE

CORNED BEEF HASH NESTS WITH EGGS

Shape 2 cups canned (15½ oz.) corned beef hash into patties. Melt 2 tablespoons butter in skillet. Cook patties slowly until browned on bottom, turn and with spoon make indentation in top of each. Place an egg in each pattie, cover skillet, continue cooking until eggs set. *Makes 4 patties.*

COLONEL CORN MUFFINS

One-half 18-oz. package (1¾ cups) Flako Corn Muffin Mix	½ cup milk
1 egg	1 can (12 oz.) whole kernel corn, drained

Preheat oven to 400° F. Grease 12 medium muffin cups. Combine mix with egg and milk, blend just until dry ingredients are thoroughly moistened. Stir in drained corn. Spoon into muffin cups, filling half full. Bake about 15 minutes or until golden brown. *Makes 12 muffins.*

FRUITED COFFEE CAKE

Prepare Aunt Jemima Coffee Cake Easy Mix batter as directed on package. After squeezing batter into the aluminum pan, sprinkle with ¼ cup chopped candied fruit; swirl lightly. Over this sprinkle topping contained in smaller bag and slivered blanched almonds. Bake as directed. *Makes 8 servings.*

SPRING WEEK-END

STRAWBERRIES WITH CREAM

HERB OMELET

*CHEDDAR APPLE COFFEE CAKE

*BANANA MUFFINS

COFFEE

CHEDDAR APPLE COFFEE CAKE

Prepare Aunt Jemima Coffee Cake Easy Mix batter as directed on package. After squeezing batter into the aluminum pan, sprinkle with ½ cup chopped apples and ½ cup grated Cheddar cheese. Over this sprinkle topping contained in smaller bag. Bake as directed. *Makes 8 servings.*

BANANA MUFFINS

2 cups Aunt Jemima Pancake Mix	1 cup milk
½ cup sugar	2 tablespoons melted shortening or oil
¼ teaspoon nutmeg	½ cup mashed banana
1 egg, beaten	

Combine pancake mix, sugar, and nutmeg in bowl; add egg, milk and shortening; stir until dry ingredients are thoroughly moistened. Stir in banana, blend well. Fill 18 greased medium muffin cups ⅔ full. Bake in oven preheated to 425° F. for 15 to 20 minutes until golden. *Makes 18 muffins.*

Overleaf—Superb brunches: Aunt Jemima Pancakes with Maple-Glazed Apple Slices, p. 19; Shrimp and Cheese Souffle, p. 23; Strawberry Birthday Cake Roll, p. 21.

SUMMER BREAKFAST

CANTALOUP HALVES

*DANISH SCRAMBLED EGG SMORREBROD

*BLUEBERRY CUP CAKES

COFFEE OR BUTTERMILK

DANISH SCRAMBLED EGG SMORREBROD

Make open-faced sandwiches using frozen Aunt Jemima Country Waffles: Heat waffles in toaster, top each hot waffle with scrambled eggs, garnish with tiny shrimp, sprats or bacon curls and slit tomato slices to stand upright atop the eggs.

BLUEBERRY CUP CAKES

1 package Flako Cup Cake Mix
1 egg
½ cup milk
1 cup fresh blueberries

Grease 12 large muffin cups. Prepare cup cake mix with egg and milk according to package directions, stir in blueberries. Spoon batter into muffin cups, filling half full. Bake in oven preheated to 350° F. about 20 to 25 minutes until golden. *Makes 12 large cup cakes.*

Cup Cake Variations: In place of blueberries in above recipe, use 1 cup well-drained crushed pineapple.

Or: Substitute 1 cup cut-up pitted dates for blueberries.

Or: Substitute ½ cup mashed, ripe bananas for the blueberries.

A breakfast for all seasons: Elegant Eggs Benedict on Waffles, recipe, p. 22; to go with Frozen Cinnamon Sticks, served fragrant and hot.

HARVEST BREAKFAST

*RAISIN–STUFFED APPLES

*EASY SAUSAGE SCRAPPLE

MILK   COFFEE

RAISIN-STUFFED APPLES

6 baking apples, peeled and cored
½ cup raisins
½ cup Aunt Jemima Syrup
1 teaspoon cinnamon
2 teaspoons butter or margarine

Place apples in baking pan, stuff raisins in cored center of each apple. Heat together syrup and cinnamon, pour over apples. Dot butter over top of each. Bake in oven preheated to 375° F. about 30 minutes or until tender. *Makes 6 servings.*

EASY SAUSAGE SCRAPPLE

1 lb. pork sausage meat
1 cup cold water or apple juice
1 cup Quaker Enriched Corn Meal (yellow or white)
2 tablespoons all-purpose flour
1½ teaspoons salt
3 cups boiling water

Pan-fry sausage until thoroughly cooked. Drain on absorbent paper. Combine water or apple juice, corn meal, flour and salt; slowly add boiling water, stirring constantly. Cook until thickened, stirring frequently. Cover; continue cooking over low heat 5 minutes, stirring occasionally. Add sausage; mix well. Pour into 8-½ x 4-½ x 2-½-inch loaf pan. Cool slightly. Cover with waxed paper, chill overnight.

When firm, cut scrapple into 12 slices. Fry on lightly greased griddle or skillet until golden. Serve warm with Aunt Jemima Syrup. *Makes 6 servings.*

Nutrition-Packed Quick Breakfasts

Good breakfasts mean brighter children and better grades, so even on the hurry-hurry-hurry mornings, make sure the youngsters go off properly fed. As for adults, dieting needn't mean skimping. Even the weight-watchers can enjoy pancakes made with skimmed milk!

SCHOOLDAY BREAKFAST

*O. J. NOG

*PEACHES AND CREAM OATMEAL

*NUTTY COFFEE CAKE

O. J. NOG

To 1 cup orange juice add 1 egg; beat 30 seconds to blend. Serve topped with a dash of nutmeg, if desired. *Makes 1 serving.*

PEACHES AND CREAM OATMEAL

½ teaspoon salt	½ cup canned sliced peaches, drained
1 cup milk	
1 cup water	
1 cup Quaker Oats (quick or old fashioned, uncooked)	

Add salt to milk and water in saucepan; bring to a boil. Stir in oats and cook, stirring occasionally, until thickened (quick oats, about 1 minute; old fashioned oats, about 5 minutes). Turn off heat, stir in peaches, cover pan, and let stand a few minutes. Serve topped with cream or half and half. *Makes 3 servings.*

NUTTY COFFEE CAKE

Prepare Aunt Jemima Coffee Cake Easy Mix according to package directions, but before adding topping, sprinkle ½ cup chopped peanuts or slivered almonds over batter. Bake as directed. *Makes 8 servings.*

ALL–IN–ONE BREAKFAST

*INSTANT CEREAL AND JUICE NOG

INSTANT CEREAL AND JUICE NOG

3 tablespoons frozen orange juice concentrate	1 cup milk
	1 egg
1 package (1 oz.) Instant Quaker Oatmeal	1 teaspoon Aunt Jemima Syrup

Combine all ingredients in blender. Beat until smooth. Sip like an egg nog. *Makes 1 serving.*

LOW-CALORIE BREAKFAST

GRAPEFRUIT JUICE

*SLIM CHEESE PANCAKES

BLACK COFFEE

SLIM CHEESE PANCAKES

½ cup Aunt Jemima Buttermilk Pancake Mix	1 tablespoon oil
	¼ cup creamed cottage cheese
⅓ cup skimmed milk	
1 egg	Low-calorie fruit preserves

Combine pancake mix, skimmed milk, egg and oil; stir until batter is fairly smooth. Bake pancakes on preheated lightly greased griddle. Serve topped with cottage cheese and low-calorie fruit preserves. *Makes 4 pancakes.*

Regional Breakfast Specialties

In New England, old Yankee traditions call for breakfast hearty enough to stick to the ribs—often with pancakes set off by tangy apples and the sweet flavor of maple. Southerners treasure grits and red-eye gravy as real he-man kind of food. Californians prefer to innovate with something new and different for the first as well as the last meals of the day. Here's a quick tour of breakfast ideas from the four corners of our country.

DIXIE SPECIAL

SLICED PEACHES AND CREAM

*HAM WITH GRITS, RED-EYE GRAVY

COFFEE

HAM WITH GRITS, RED-EYE GRAVY

1 cup Quaker Enriched White Hominy Grits	1 center slice of ham
5 cups boiling water*	1 tablespoon butter or margarine
1 teaspoon salt	¾ cup strong coffee

Prepare grits according to package directions in boiling salted water. Fry ham in butter; remove and cut into serving pieces. Brown drippings over high heat, then add coffee, bring to a boil, cook 1 minute. Pour gravy into gravy boat. Serve ham and gravy with the cooked grits. *Makes 6 servings.*

Note: To use quick grits, decrease water to 4 cups. Cook uncovered 2½ to 5 minutes, stirring occasionally.

YANKEE EYE-OPENER

*MAPLE-GLAZED APPLE SLICES

*CHEESE SCRAMBLED EGGS

*BUCKWHEAT CAKES WITH SAUSAGE COINS

COFFEE   TEA

MAPLE-GLAZED APPLE SLICES

Pictured on page 14.

Core 2 or 3 firm tart apples; slice thickly. Sauté in 2 tablespoons butter or margarine until lightly browned on one side. Turn; add ½ cup Aunt Jemima Syrup, cook until apple slices are nicely glazed. Serve over Aunt Jemima Pancakes.

CHEESE SCRAMBLED EGGS

Prepare scrambled eggs in your usual way, sprinkling shredded American or Cheddar cheese over eggs when half cooked.

BUCKWHEAT CAKES WITH SAUSAGE COINS

Brown and serve sausage links	1 egg
1 cup Aunt Jemima Buckwheat Pancake Mix	1 tablespoon melted sausage or bacon drippings
1 cup milk	

Cut sausage links in thick slices. Arrange slices in clusters on preheated griddle or skillet. Combine pancake mix, milk, egg and melted drippings. Pour batter over sausage clusters. Turn when tops are covered with bubbles and edges look cooked. Turn only once. *Makes about 12 pancakes.*

CALIFORNIA CALLING

FRESH STRAWBERRIES

*CHICKEN PANCAKES WITH ORANGE SYRUP

COFFEE

CHICKEN PANCAKES

2 eggs
1½ cups milk
2 cups Aunt Jemima
  Buttermilk Pancake Mix
¼ cup melted butter or
  margarine

1 cup diced cooked or
  canned chicken
¼ cup diced pitted dates
  (optional)

Beat eggs until light and fluffy. Blend in milk. Add pancake mix, stir just until thoroughly moistened. Stir in melted butter, chicken, and dates. Bake pancakes on a hot griddle in the usual way. Serve with Orange Syrup (see below). *Makes 18–20 pancakes, 4 inches in diameter.*

ORANGE SYRUP

1 large navel orange
3 tablespoons butter or
  margarine

¾ cup Aunt Jemima Syrup

Carefully peel orange, removing only outermost peel. Cut peel into slivers, enough to make 2 tablespoons. Remove all white membrane from orange, cut orange in small pieces. Sauté the slivered orange peel and the diced orange in butter about 1 minute, until lightly browned. Add the syrup, cook 1 minute longer. Serve hot over the pancakes. *Makes about 1 cup.*

MIDWESTERN MORN

STEWED PRUNES

FRIED EGGS AND BACON

*FRIED MUSH

FRIED MUSH

Heat to boiling 3 cups water in saucepan. Mix 1 cup Quaker Yellow Corn Meal and 1 teaspoon salt with 1 cup cold water. Pour into the boiling water, stirring constantly. Cook until thickened, stirring frequently. Cover; continue cooking over low heat 10 minutes or longer. Pour cooked corn meal into loaf pan. When cold, cut into ½-inch slices; pan-fry slowly on lightly greased griddle or skillet until golden brown. Serve hot with Aunt Jemima Syrup. *Makes 6 servings.*

TOUCH OF THE TROPICS

TROPICAL JUICE COCKTAIL

*HAWAIIAN SUNRISE PANCAKES

HAWAIIAN SUNRISE PANCAKES

One-half 18-oz. package
  (1¾ cups) Flako Corn
  Muffin Mix
1 egg, beaten
1 cup milk
1 tablespoon butter or
  margarine, melted

½ cup crushed pineapple,
  well-drained
4 eggs, fried in butter
Chutney (optional)

Combine muffin mix, beaten egg, milk and melted butter; stir in drained crushed pineapple. Pour batter on hot, lightly greased griddle as for pancakes, making cakes about 4 inches in diameter; turn when golden. Place an egg on each serving of pancakes, with chutney as a topping, if desired. *Makes 4 servings.*

Special Occasion Breakfasts and Brunches

Be just a little dramatic when company's coming for breakfast. It makes for a fun kind of party when you serve spiced banana muffins with scrambled eggs, or glorify the breakfast table with a feathery-light soufflé. Celebrate holidays and special anniversaries with foods appropriate to the occasion, such as corn bread baked in a heart for Valentine's, and red-white-and-blue compote for Fourth of July. The better the day, the more important the breakfast, so cook it up.

BIRTHDAY BREAKFAST

APRICOT NECTAR

*PIPERADE

*MAPLE TOAST

*STRAWBERRY BIRTHDAY CAKE ROLL

COFFEE   MILK

PIPERADE

½ green pepper, cut in thin strips
3 tablespoons olive or salad oil
1 small onion, minced
1 tomato, peeled and chopped

¼ cup minced cooked ham
1 teaspoon salt
8 eggs, beaten until light

Sauté green pepper in oil until lightly browned; add onion, cook until soft. Add tomato and ham, cook until tomato is soft and ham lightly browned. Sprinkle mixture with salt. Reduce heat, add half the eggs, lifting up and over with spatula until firm but still moist. Add remaining eggs. As soon as mixture is firm throughout, cut into serving portions and serve on warmed plates. *Makes 6 servings.*

MAPLE TOAST

Spread hot toast with Maple Butter: Beat 1 cup butter until light and fluffy, then gradually beat in ½ cup Aunt Jemima Syrup.

STRAWBERRY BIRTHDAY CAKE ROLL

Pictured on page 15.

1 pint fresh strawberries
1 cup granulated sugar
2 tablespoons butter or margarine
3 eggs
1 teaspoon lemon juice or vanilla extract

⅔ cup Aunt Jemima Pancake Mix
Confectioners sugar
1 cup heavy cream, whipped

Preheat oven to 400° F. Reserve 6 to 8 berries for garnish. Chop and sweeten remaining berries with ¼ cup of the sugar. Melt butter over low heat just until liquified. Beat eggs until frothy; beat in remaining ¾ cup sugar. Stir in melted butter, lemon juice or vanilla extract and the pancake mix. Grease a 15x10-inch jelly roll pan. Cover bottom of pan with waxed paper; grease again and flour. Pour in batter. Bake about 10 minutes until golden. Immediately turn out on towel well-sprinkled with confectioners sugar. Carefully pull off paper from cake. Roll up with towel and cool about 20 minutes. Unroll and spread cake with whipped cream and the chopped berries. Roll cake up quickly. Sprinkle more confectioners sugar over the top. Serve with reserved berries as garnish. *Makes 1 cake roll.*

SHOWER BRUNCH

*CRAN-ORANGE FRAPPÉ

*EGGS BENEDICT ON WAFFLES

*DESSERT ROLL WITH RUM-FLAVORED
WHIPPED CREAM

COFFEE

CRAN-ORANGE FRAPPÉ

Combine equal parts cranberry juice and orange juice. Serve chilled.

EGGS BENEDICT ON WAFFLES

Pictured on page 16.

Heat frozen Aunt Jemima Country Waffles in toaster, 2 per serving. To serve, top 2 waffle sections with a thin slice of ham, 2 poached eggs and Hollandaise Sauce.

DESSERT ROLL WITH
RUM-FLAVORED WHIPPED CREAM

1 cup Aunt Jemima Buttermilk Pancake Mix	2 tablespoons butter or margarine, melted
1¼ cups milk	Rum-flavored whipped cream (see below)
1 egg	

Combine pancake mix, milk, egg and melted butter. Beat until smooth. Pour batter into a 10-inch skillet with sloping sides. When bubbles form all over top, turn using two pancake turners. Bake on the other side. Remove to towel sprinkled with confectioners sugar, roll loosely, let cool 20 minutes. Unroll and carefully transfer to serving dish, fill with rum-flavored whipped cream, fold over. Sprinkle top with confectioners sugar and spoon fresh berries or other fresh fruit over the top.

Rum-flavored Whipped Cream. Beat 1 cup heavy cream until thick. Fold in 2 tablespoons confectioners sugar and 2 tablespoons golden rum.

HIKER'S BREAKFAST

BANANAS OR APPLES

*FRANKFURTER AND EGG SCRAMBLE

*JOHNNYCAKES

COCOA TOPPED WITH MARSHMALLOW

FRANKFURTER AND EGG SCRAMBLE

Slice frankfurters. Sauté in butter or margarine in skillet until lightly browned. Add beaten eggs, scramble with fork before they can set. Sprinkle with salt and pepper.

JOHNNYCAKES

1 package (12 oz.) Flako Corn Muffin Mix	2 eggs
1 cup instant nonfat dry milk solids	1 cup water

Combine corn muffin mix and dry milk solids before starting off on hiking trip. To prepare at campsite, add eggs and water, stir until dry ingredients are thoroughly moistened. Cook like pancakes on lightly greased griddle or skillet, but these will be thicker than pancakes, more like scones. Eat with fingers like muffins. *Makes about 12 cakes.*

FRIENDSHIP BRUNCH

FRUIT SALAD IN MELON BASKET

*SHRIMP AND CHEESE SOUFFLE

TOASTED ENGLISH MUFFINS, MAPLE BUTTER

COFFEE

SHRIMP AND CHEESE SOUFFLE
Pictured on page 14.

6 eggs, separated	1 cup milk
¼ cup Aunt Jemima Pancake Mix	¾ cup shredded sharp cheese
½ teaspoon salt	1 can (about 4½ oz.) shrimp drained, minced
Pinch of cayenne pepper	

Beat egg yolks until thick and lemon colored. Place pancake mix, salt and cayenne in medium-sized saucepan. Gradually stir in milk. Cook, stirring constantly until thickened. Remove from heat. Add small amount of hot mixture to beaten egg yolks. Stir egg yolk mixture into hot mixture. Add cheese and shrimp. Beat egg whites until stiff peaks form. Gently, but quickly fold several spoonfuls of beaten egg white into egg yolk mixture. Gently fold egg yolk mixture into egg whites. Pour into greased 1½ quart casserole. Bake uncovered in preheated 350° F. oven 50 to 60 minutes. *Makes 6 servings.*

CHRISTMAS BREAKFAST

FRUIT BOWL OF TANGERINES AND RED TOKAY GRAPES

*SAUSAGE PANCAKES WITH HOT APRICOT SYRUP

*CHRISTMAS CANDLE LOAVES

SAUSAGE PANCAKES WITH HOT APRICOT SYRUP

Prepare pancakes with Aunt Jemima Pancake Mix according to directions. Sprinkle cooked, drained sausage meat over pancakes before turning. Serve with hot apricot syrup. Combine ¾ cup Aunt Jemima Syrup with one jar (12 oz.) apricot preserves; bring just to a boil. Serve at once.

CHRISTMAS CANDLE LOAVES

1½ cups sifted all-purpose flour	¾ cup Quaker Oats (quick or old fashioned, uncooked)
½ cup sugar	⅓ cup milk
2 teaspoons baking powder	¼ cup salad oil
1 teaspoon salt	2 eggs, beaten
½ teaspoon soda	⅔ cup mashed banana
½ cup chopped nutmeats	Confectioners Glaze

Sift together flour, sugar, baking powder, salt and soda. Add nutmeats and oats, stir to blend. Add remaining ingredients, stir just until flour mixture is well moistened. Pour into 6 buttered and floured empty juice cans (6 oz. size). Bake in oven preheated to 350° F. for 30 minutes, until golden and firm. Let stand 5 minutes; remove from cans; cool thoroughly. (These should be made two days in advance.) Wrap cooled bread; store one day, then unwrap, dribble Confectioners Glaze over top and down the sides of each to resemble dripping candle wax. Stick a thin gumdrop in top of each for "wick". *Makes 6 individual loaves.*

Confectioners Glaze. To 1 cup confectioners sugar add milk, 1 teaspoon at a time, until mixture is consistency of cream. Spread or dribble with spoon at once over cake.

VALENTINE'S DAY

CRANBERRY JUICE

*ROSY SCRAMBLED EGGS
WITH BACON

*CORN BREAD HEART

COCOA

ROSY SCRAMBLED EGGS WITH BACON

1 large tomato, peeled, chopped	⅛ teaspoon pepper
1 tablespoons butter or margarine	1 tablespoon milk or cream
½ teaspoon salt	6 eggs, beaten
	8 slices crisp cooked bacon

Sauté the tomato in butter 4 or 5 minutes; sprinkle with ¼ teaspoon of the salt and pepper. Stir milk or cream into eggs with remaining salt. Add ½ of the egg mixture to skillet; lift up and over as it firms. Add remaining egg mixture. As soon as all of egg mixture is cooked but still slightly moist, serve immediately, with 2 slices of bacon for each serving. *Makes 4 servings.*

CORN BREAD HEART

Prepare corn bread with Flako Corn Muffin Mix (12 oz. package) according to directions for making corn muffins, but bake in a greased 5-cup heart shaped mold in an oven preheated to 400° F. until browned, about 20 to 25 minutes.

EASTER BRUNCH

EGGNOG

*PUFFY HAM PANCAKES WITH SPICED SYRUP

STRAWBERRY CHEESE PIE

COFFEE

PUFFY HAM PANCAKES

1 cup Aunt Jemima Pancake Mix	1 tablespoon melted shortening
1 cup milk	1 cup minced cooked ham
2 egg yolks	2 egg whites, stiffly beaten

Place pancake mix, milk, egg yolks and shortening in bowl. Stir until dry ingredients are thoroughly moistened. Add ham, blend well. Fold in egg whites. Bake pancakes in the usual way, pouring ¼ cup batter onto hot griddle for each pancake. Serve hot with Spiced Syrup (see below).

Spiced Syrup. Add ¼ teaspoon cloves, 1 teaspoon prepared mustard, and 1 tablespoon butter to ½ cup Aunt Jemima Syrup. Heat until butter melts. Pour hot syrup over Puffy Ham Pancakes.

JULY FOURTH BREAKFAST

*RED, WHITE AND BLUE COMPOTE

SHIRRED EGGS

*CHEESE AND BACON UPSIDE DOWN CORN BREAD

BUTTER   JAM

MILK   COFFEE

RED, WHITE AND BLUE COMPOTE

Arrange strawberries or raspberries and blueberries in glass bowl; serve topped with cream.

CHEESE AND BACON
UPSIDE DOWN CORN BREAD

6 slices bacon, partially cooked	1 egg
	½ cup milk
1 package Aunt Jemima Corn Bread Easy Mix	½ cup shredded American or Cheddar cheese

Drain partially cooked bacon on absorbent paper, then place in the special aluminum foil pan that comes in the package of mix. Prepare batter according to package directions, pour over bacon in pan. Sprinkle cheese over the batter. Bake in oven preheated to 425° F. about 20 minutes until golden. Turn out of pan to serve, so that bacon is on top. *Makes 6 servings.*

THANKSGIVING BREAKFAST

SPICED TOMATO JUICE

BACON AND EGGS

*CRANBERRY CORN MUFFINS

*PUMPKIN COFFEE CAKE

COFFEE   MILK

CRANBERRY CORN MUFFINS

Prepare muffins with Flako Corn Muffin Mix according to package directions. After batter has been poured into muffin cups, place a scant teaspoon of whole cranberry sauce in top of each. Bake as directed.

PUMPKIN COFFEE CAKE

Prepare Aunt Jemima Coffee Cake Easy Mix batter according to package directions, adding to the large bag of mix ½ cup canned pumpkin and ¼ teaspoon allspice along with egg and milk. Sprinkle topping over batter, bake as directed. *Makes 8 servings.*

ANNIVERSARY BREAKFAST

ORANGE AND PINEAPPLE SLICES

*CURRIED OMELET

CORN STICKS

*BANANA BEIGNETS

VIENNESE COFFEE

CURRIED OMELET

Prepare omelet as usual, adding a pinch of curry powder (more or less, according to taste) to the beaten egg.

BANANA BEIGNETS

1 cup Aunt Jemima Pancake Mix	6 large bananas, cut in 1-inch pieces
1 egg, beaten	Fat or oil for deep fat frying
½ cup milk	

Combine pancake mix, egg and milk, mix until batter is fairly smooth. Let stand 5 minutes. Dip pieces of banana in batter; chill while fat is heating. Fry in hot deep fat heated to 375° F. until golden on all sides. Drain on absorbent paper. Serve hot with syrup. *Makes 8 servings.*

CHAPTER III

Lunches and Meals on the Go

What makes a light meal memorable? Whether it's a simple sandwich-and-soup lunch, or a card party spread, a picnic basket to be opened on beach or in woodland retreat, or a stay-for-a-bite waffle stack, little extras make the difference. Think of contrasting color and texture, something hot with cool salads, something cool and refreshing to follow a hot entree. Add an unusual bread or prepare a favorite dish, and in a subtle way you are saying this has been prepared with individual thought and care.

Waffle-A-Lunch

Here's a trio of quick, dress-up ideas for meal-in-one hot open sandwiches which use waffles as a base. Use waffles which go from freezer to toaster in one quick motion, or prepare your own with ease, using a waffle mix.

COME TO LUNCHEON

*CREAMED SHRIMP AND PEAS

WAFFLES

WATERCRESS SALAD

*FROZEN RASPBERRY PARFAIT

CREAMED SHRIMP AND PEAS

1 lb. shelled and deveined raw shrimp

2 tablespoons slivered blanched almonds

2 tablespoons butter or margarine

1 can (10 oz.) frozen condensed cream of shrimp soup, thawed

⅓ cup milk or sherry

1 cup cooked peas

8 frozen Aunt Jemima Country Waffles

Sauté the shrimp and almonds in butter over low heat just until pink. Add soup, milk or sherry and cooked peas. Cook over low heat 3 or 4 minutes. Prepare waffles in toaster or oven according to package directions. Serve hot creamed sauce on waffles. *Makes 4 servings.*

FROZEN RASPBERRY PARFAIT

Layer vanilla ice cream and defrosted frozen raspberries (well-drained) in parfait glasses. Top with whipped cream. Keep in freezer until time to serve.

TURKEY WAFFLE LUNCH

*TURKEY DIVAN OPEN SANDWICH

*EASY LEMON BAVARIAN

**LACE COOKIES
See page 104.

TURKEY DIVAN OPEN SANDWICH

Pictured on page 29.

Mornay Sauce (see below)

1 package (10 oz.) frozen broccoli spears, cooked

8 slices cooked turkey white meat

8 frozen Aunt Jemima Country Waffles

In advance, prepare Mornay Sauce, cook broccoli, and cut turkey in thick (¼ inch) slices. Shortly before serving, toast waffles. Arrange broccoli spears over waffles, top with 2 turkey slices, and cover with Mornay Sauce. Place under broiler until sauce is lightly browned. *Makes 4 servings.*

Mornay Sauce. Melt 2 tablespoons butter or margarine in skillet, add 1 teaspoon minced or finely sliced white onion, cook until onion is yellow. Add 2 tablespoons all-purpose flour, cook until mixture bubbles. Slowly stir in 1 cup milk, cook over low heat until thickened and smooth. Add ¼ cup shredded Swiss or Gruyere cheese; cook, stirring, until cheese is melted. *Makes 1 cup.*

EASY LEMON BAVARIAN

Prepare lemon pudding or pie filling mix (3 oz. package) according to package directions. Cool. Beat 2 egg whites until stiff; fold into pudding. Pour into 3-cup glass dish or individual dishes. Chill. Serve topped with whipped cream. *Makes 4–5 servings.*

GRILLED TRIPLE TREAT

*BACON-CHEESE-AND-TOMATO WAFFLE

BROILED MUSHROOM CAPS

*FLORIDA FRUIT CUP

BACON-CHEESE-AND-TOMATO WAFFLE

6 frozen Aunt Jemima Country Waffles	12 cooked bacon slices
6 tomato slices	6 slices American cheese

Heat waffles in toaster. Place on baking sheet. Top each waffle with a tomato slice, 2 bacon slices and a slice of cheese. Place under broiler until cheese melts. *Makes 3 servings.*

FLORIDA FRUIT CUP

Dice or cut up a mixture of fresh seasonal fruits, such as melon balls, fresh strawberries, pineapple wedges, bananas or apples. Arrange in sherbet dishes. Cover each serving with mixture of ¼ cup orange juice and 1 tablespoon Aunt Jemima Syrup. Chill until serving time.

Salad Bowl Specials

COOL BUT SATISFYING

*MEAT-AND-POTATOES SALAD

TOASTED GARLIC BREAD

PINEAPPLE WEDGES MARINATED IN GINGER ALE

*COCONUT DREAM BARS

COFFEE

MEAT-AND-POTATOES SALAD

6 slices (about ½ lb.) rare roast beef, cut in thin slivers	1 quart salad greens, torn in bite-sized pieces
½ cup clear French dressing	4 anchovy filets, drained, chopped
3 medium potatoes, cooked, peeled, diced	4 hard-cooked eggs, cut in slivers
3 cups young green beans, cooked until just tender	

Marinate beef in half the French dressing. Marinate potatoes and beans in remaining dressing. Store salad greens in vegetable freshener until needed. Shortly before serving, combine all ingredients, toss to blend. *Makes 6 servings.*

COCONUT DREAM BARS

Butterscotch Base:	*Coconut Topping:*
⅓ cup soft shortening	2 eggs
⅓ cup firmly packed brown sugar	1 cup firmly packed brown sugar
¾ cup sifted all-purpose flour	1 tablespoon all-purpose flour
½ teaspoon soda	1 tablespoon lemon juice
½ teaspoon salt	Grated peel of 1 lemon
¾ cup Quaker Oats (quick or old fashioned, uncooked)	1 cup shredded coconut
	½ cup chopped pecans

For base, beat shortening and sugar together until creamy. Sift together flour, soda and salt. Add to creamed mixture; blend well. Stir in oats. (This mixture will be very dry and crumbly.) Pat into greased 11 x 7-inch baking pan.

For topping, beat eggs slightly. Blend in remaining ingredients. Pour over base. Bake in oven preheated to 350° F. about 30 minutes. Cool; cut in bars. *Makes 20 bars.*

Luncheon-perfect Turkey Divan Open Sandwich (p. 27) on Frozen Waffles—an unexpected treat that combines classic French with modern American.

THE PACIFIC INFLUENCE

*CALIFORNIA STYLE
SHRIMP SALAD WITH GREEN GODDESS DRESSING

**ORANGE NUT BREAD
See page 91.

*MAPLE NUT SUNDAE

CALIFORNIA-STYLE SHRIMP SALAD

1 lb. shelled and deveined shrimp, cooked	Salad greens
½ cup sliced celery	2 hard-cooked eggs, cut in thin wedges
¼ cup slivered green pepper	Black pitted olives for garnish
Juice of 1 lemon	Green Goddess Dressing (see below)
¼ teaspoon salt	

Combine shrimp, celery and green pepper. Sprinkle with lemon juice and salt; chill until serving time. Shortly before serving, arrange salad greens on each plate, top with shrimp mixture, arrange egg wedges and black olives over shrimp for garnish. Pass the Green Goddess Dressing. *Makes 4 luncheon servings.*

GREEN GODDESS DRESSING

1 clove garlic	½ cup dairy sour cream
2 tablespoons minced anchovies	2 tablespoons minced chives
1 tablespoon tarragon vinegar	¼ cup minced fresh parsley
1 cup mayonnaise	Freshly ground black pepper

Salad bowl specials, crisp and cool Chef Caesar Salad, recipe, p. 31; Tomato Rose with Crabmeat Salad, p. 33; Aunt Jemima Frozen Corn Sticks, toasted hot.

Mash garlic in small mixing bowl with back of spoon; discard shreds. Add remaining ingredients to bowl, blend. Refrigerate ½ to 1 hour before serving. *Makes about 1½ cups.*

MAPLE NUT SUNDAE

Serve vanilla ice cream topped with Aunt Jemima Syrup and chopped nuts (peanuts, walnuts or pecans).

SALAD TO A MAN'S TASTE

*CHEF CAESAR SALAD

CORN STICKS

LEMON SHERBET WITH
COCONUT TOPPING

ICED TEA

CHEF CAESAR SALAD

Pictured on page 30.

1 or 2 garlic cloves	1 cup slivered Swiss cheese
½ cup salad oil	1 or 2 tomatoes, cut in wedges
2 quarts salad greens, in bite-size pieces	1 can (2 oz.) anchovies
1 cup slivered cooked ham	Salt and pepper
1 cup slivered cooked chicken or turkey	Juice of 1 lemon
	1 egg, raw or coddled
	1 cup croutons

Place garlic in small bowl, crush with back of spoon, add salad oil; let stand 1 hour. Arrange salad bowl with greens, ham, chicken, cheese and tomatoes. Add anchovies and garlic-flavored oil; sprinkle with salt and pepper. Toss to blend lightly. Add lemon juice and egg, toss again until egg disappears. Add croutons. Prepare frozen Aunt Jemima Corn Sticks according to package directions. Serve with Chef Caesar Salad. *Makes 6–8 servings.*

TEMPTINGLY DIFFERENT

*TOMATO ROSE WITH CRAB MEAT

*GRITS SOUFFLE

*HOT BANANA SUNDAE

TOMATO ROSE WITH CRAB MEAT
Pictured on page 30.

6 large tomatoes	½ cup mayonnaise
1 large green pepper	2 tablespoons catsup
1½ cups flaked crab meat	1 teaspoon lemon juice
1 cup minced celery	Salt and pepper to taste
1 tablespoon minced onion or scallions	Lettuce cups

Slash each tomato in 6 sections, cutting almost to the base. Spread out. Sprinkle with salt. Cut 6 horizontal rings from the pepper. Mince remaining green pepper, add to mixture of crab meat, celery, minced onion, mayonnaise, tomato catsup, and lemon juice. Season to taste. Spoon crabmeat mixture into tomatoes, using green pepper rings as garnish. Place stuffed tomatoes on lettuce cups. Chill. *Makes 6 servings.*

GRITS SOUFFLÉ

3 tablespoons hot milk	3 eggs, separated
2 tablespoons minced onion	½ cup grated sharp cheese
½ teaspoon salt	
1 cup freshly cooked Quaker Enriched White Hominy Grits	

Add milk, onion and salt to grits. Beat egg yolks until thick and lemon-colored; stir egg yolks and

Pack up and go! From the picnic hamper, Tamale Loaf, recipe, p. 37; Cheese-filled Surprise Burgers, p. 35. In basket, Maple Syrup Cookies, p. 36.

cheese into grits mixture. Beat egg whites until stiff; fold into grits mixture. Pour into *ungreased* 1-quart casserole or soufflé dish with straight sides. Set in baking pan, add boiling water to pan to depth of 1 inch. Bake in oven preheated to 350° F. about 1 hour until golden. Serve immediately. *Makes 6 servings.*

HOT BANANA SUNDAE

Slice bananas lengthwise, sauté in butter or margarine until lightly browned on each side; add a tablespoon or two of Aunt Jemima Syrup. Serve warm over vanilla ice cream.

TROPICAL BUFFET

*POLYNESIAN FRUIT SALAD

*CRUNCHY GRITS BISCUITS

**LIME CHIFFON PIE
See page 107

POLYNESIAN FRUIT SALAD

1 ripe pineapple	½ green pepper, cut in slivers
1 seedless orange, peeled, diced	1 large banana, cut in cubes
1 cup diced cooked ham	Polynesian Dressing (page 34)

Cut pineapple lengthwise to form boat shape: scoop out fruit from center to ½ inch from edge. Core and dice fruit, combine with orange, ham, green pepper and banana. Marinate salad mixture in Polynesian Dressing until shortly before time to serve, then spoon into pineapple "boat." Serve from the pineapple shell. *Makes about 8 servings.*

POLYNESIAN DRESSING

1 tablespoon soy sauce	¼ teaspoon ground ginger
2 tablespoons Aunt Jemima Syrup	½ cup orange juice
1 tablespoon prepared mustard	2 to 3 tablespoons oil

Combine all ingredients; shake or beat to blend. Use with fruit salad. *Makes about 1 cup.*

CRUNCHY GRITS BISCUITS

1½ cups sifted all-purpose flour	¼ cup shortening
4 teaspoons baking powder	¼ cup chopped green onion
1 teaspoon salt	1 cup grated sharp cheese
½ cup Quaker Enriched White Hominy Grits (quick or regular)	½ cup milk

Sift together flour, baking powder, and salt; stir in grits, reserving 1 tablespoon. Cut in shortening until mixture resembles coarse crumbs. Stir in onion and cheese. Gradually add milk, stirring until all dry ingredients are moistened and mixture can be formed into soft dough. Knead lightly. Sprinkle pastry board with flour and reserved 1 tablespoon grits. Roll out dough to form rectangle 8 x 9-inches. Cut into 8 strips, each 1 inch wide, then cut each strip into 3 pieces, each 3 inches long. Place 1 inch apart on ungreased baking sheet. Bake in oven preheated to 425° F. for 10 to 12 minutes until lightly browned. Serve hot. *Makes 2 dozen.*

FOR THE FEMININE TOUCH

*FRUIT SALAD PLATTER,

*ORANGE CREAM DRESSING

POPOVERS

*HOT SPICED TEA

FRUIT SALAD PLATTER

Arrange on a platter, or individual plates, an assortment of seasonal fruit selected for contrasting colors and textures. For example, seeded watermelon cubes, blueberries, orange segments and cubes of banana (sprinkled with lemon juice to avoid darkening). Or combine diced apple, seeded grapes, Mandarin orange or tangerine segments and bananas. Serve with Orange Cream Dressing (see below).

ORANGE CREAM DRESSING

1 package (3 oz.) cream cheese, softened	1 tablespoon orange juice
	¼ cup Aunt Jemima Syrup

Combine cheese and orange juice, beat in syrup until smooth. *Makes about ½ cup, or 4 servings.*

HOT SPICED TEA

3 tea bags	⅓ cup sugar
1 (3-inch) stick of cinnamon; or ½ teaspoon cinnamon	1 teaspoon grated lemon peel
10 whole cloves	¼ cup fresh lemon juice
6 cups boiling water	Lemon quarters or slices

Place tea bags in heated large teapot; add spices loosely tied in cheese cloth. Pour boiling water over tea; cover, steep 5 minutes. Remove spice bag and tea bags; add sugar, grated lemon peel and fresh lemon juice. Serve hot with lemon slices. *Makes 8–10 cups.*

Pack-Up-and-Go Lunches

There's a new mobility to meals—served on trays or TV tables, moved out to the patio, transported in hampers to a picnic spot with a view. New featherweight insulated containers and gaily-decorated paper products make mobile meals easier than ever to transport, daintier and easier to serve. Even school lunch boxes can be packed with delicious surprises. Instead of routine peanut butter and jelly sandwiches, prepare savory turnovers or hearty meal-in-a-bun Heroes, with crunchy Maple Syrup Cookies or Cinnamon Pinwheels to send a child back to class well fed and happy.

PICNIC HAMPER

*MANHATTAN CHOWDER JUG

*SURPRISE CHEESEBURGERS

WATERMELON

LEMONADE

MANHATTAN CHOWDER JUG

1 stalk celery, minced	1 soup can water
1 tablespoon butter or margarine	2 cans (7 oz. each) minced clams and juice
½ teaspoon thyme	
1 can (10¾ oz.) condensed tomato soup	

Sauté celery in butter with thyme until soft; add condensed soup, water and clams and juice; bring just to a boil. Pour into thermos jug. At picnic site, serve in hot-drink paper cups. *Makes 8 servings.*

SURPRISE CHEESEBURGERS

Pictured on page 32.

1½ lbs. ground beef	½ cup milk
¾ cup Quaker Oats (quick or old fashioned	1 jar (5 oz.) process cheese spread
1 teaspoon instant minced onion	2 tablespoons sweet pickle relish
1½ teaspoons salt	2 teaspoons prepared mustard
¼ teaspoon pepper	
2 tablespoons catsup	

Combine beef, oats, onion, salt, pepper, catsup and milk; mix lightly, shape into 12 thin patties. Blend cheese, relish and mustard; spread as filling over 6 patties, top with remaining patties, pinch edges together to seal. Broil 4 inches from heat about 7 minutes on first side, 5 minutes on second side. Serve on toasted hamburger buns. *Makes 6 servings.*

LUNCH BOX SPECIAL

*HERO SANDWICHES

PICKLES AND CHERRY TOMATOES

*CINNAMON PINWHEELS

MILK

HERO SANDWICHES

For each serving, slice Hero bun lengthwise. Pull out soft center, fill with layers of Swiss cheese, sweet pickle relish, sliced ham or salami, mustard or mayonnaise, sliced tomato, sliced red Bermuda onion; sprinkle French dressing over ingredients, put bun back together, wrap in plastic or foil.

CINNAMON PINWHEELS

Prepare 1 package Flako Pie Crust Mix according to package directions, or pastry for 2-crust pie. Divide dough in four portions, roll out each to form a 4 x 6-inch rectangle, spread each rectangle with softened butter, then sprinkle with cinnamon-sugar and raisins, dot with butter. Roll up lengthwise like jelly roll, moisten overlapped edge of pastry and press together to seal. Cut each rectangle into six 1-inch slices. Place pinwheels on ungreased baking sheet, bake in oven preheated to 425° F. until golden, about 20 minutes. *Makes about 24 pinwheels.*

LUNCHBOX SURPRISE

*TUNA TURNOVERS

APPLES

*MAPLE SYRUP COOKIES

TUNA TURNOVERS

1 can (6½ or 7 oz.) tuna, undrained	¼ cup chopped peanuts
½ cup minced celery or green pepper	1 egg, beaten
1 teaspoon instant minced onion	¼ cup milk
¼ teaspoon salt	1 package Flako Pie Crust Mix, or pastry for 2-crust pie

Combine tuna, celery or green pepper, onion, salt, peanuts, egg and milk; stir to blend. Prepare pie crust mix as directed on package (or your favorite recipe). Roll out to form a 12 x 16-inch rectangle; cut into 12 squares 4 x 4 inches each. Place a heaping tablespoon of tuna mixture in each square, fold over into a triangle, moisten and seal edges. Place turnovers on ungreased baking sheet. Preheat oven to 400° F., bake turnovers until golden, about 25 minutes. *Makes 12 turnovers.*

MAPLE SYRUP COOKIES

Pictured on page 32.

½ cup shortening, soft	½ teaspoon salt
¾ cup Aunt Jemima Syrup	1½ teaspoons baking powder
1 egg	1½ cups Quaker Oats (quick or old fashioned, uncooked)
½ teaspoon vanilla	
½ teaspoon almond extract	
1½ cups sifted all-purpose flour	½ cup chopped nutmeats

Beat shortening until creamy. Add syrup gradually, beating constantly. Blend in egg, vanilla and almond extract. Sift together flour, salt and baking powder. Add to creamed mixture, mixing well. Stir in oats and nutmeats. Drop by teaspoonfuls onto greased baking sheets. Bake in oven preheated to 375° F. about 12 to 15 minutes. *Makes 3½ dozen cookies.*

PATIO PARTY

*GAZPACHO

*TAMALE LOAF

CHERRY TARTS

ICED TEA

GAZPACHO

1 large or 2 small garlic cloves	1 can (1 lb. 14 oz.) whole peeled tomatoes
2 tablespoons minced onion	1 tablespoon vinegar
2 tablespoons chopped green pepper or 1 canned pimiento, drained	2 cups water or chicken broth
1 teaspoon salt	Minced cucumber, celery, green pepper and onion for garnish
¼ cup olive oil	
1 slice white bread	

Combine garlic, onion, green pepper or pimiento; chop fine with sharp knife or mince in blender (turning on, off, on, off 3 times). Add salt, olive oil and bread; beat until paste-like. Add the canned tomatoes straining through a sieve; beat until very smooth. Add blended mixture to vinegar and water or broth, chill several hours or overnight. Serve very cold in soup bowls garnished with minced raw vegetables. *Makes 6–8 servings.*

TAMALE LOAF

Pictured on page 32

¾ lb. ground beef
1 tablespoon fat or oil
1 small onion, chopped
1 tablespoon chili powder
1 small green pepper, seeded, chopped
¼ cup chili sauce
1 can (15 oz.) chili with beans

1 package Aunt Jemima Corn Bread Easy Mix
6 to 8 stuffed olives

Wax-paper line and grease 8½x4½x2½-inch loaf pan. Sauté beef in fat, stirring until it loses pink color. Drain off excess fat. Add onion, chili powder and chopped green pepper; cook until onion is soft. Add chili sauce and chili. Cook 15 to 20 minutes. Prepare corn bread according to directions; spread ½ of batter into prepared loaf pan, cover with the meat mixture. Gently spread remaining ½ batter over the meat mixture. Place olive halves over batter for garnish. Bake in oven preheated to 425°F. 20 to 25 minutes or until corn bread is browned. Cool slightly about 10 minutes before turning out of pans. Cut in thick slices to serve. *Makes 6 servings.*

Special Occasion Luncheons

Guests of all ages like food with a flair. An oat biscuit crust on tuna casserole, a frothy Maple Velvet Pie, the touch of curry in a grits ring help turn an ordinary luncheon into an exotic repast.

RING-A-ROUND LUNCH

*CURRIED GRITS RING WITH CREAMED TURKEY

TOSSED VEGETABLE SALAD

DEVIL'S FOOD CAKE A LA MODE

CURRIED GRITS RING

⅓ cup chopped onion
¾ cup diced celery
1 tablespoon curry powder
¼ cup butter or margarine
5 cups chicken broth
1 teaspoon salt
⅛ teaspoon pepper

1 tablespoon chopped parsley
¼ bay leaf
¼ teaspoon thyme
1¼ cups Quaker Enriched White Hominy Grits*

Cook onion, celery and curry powder in butter 5 minutes. Add broth, bring to a boil. Add seasonings and slowly stir in grits. Cover, cook over low heat 25 to 30 minutes, stirring frequently. Remove bay leaf. Pour into 6-cup (1½ quart) ring mold. Let stand at room temperature about 20 minutes, then cover and refrigerate several hours or overnight. To reheat, place mold on a rack in large pan; pour water around mold to depth of 2 inches. Cover; bring to a boil, steam 20 to 25 minutes. Remove ring mold from water, unmold on platter. Fill with *Creamed Turkey, page 39. Makes 6 servings.*

To use quick grits, increase grits to 1½ cups. Cook uncovered 2½ to 5 minutes, stirring occasionally.

SCOUT LEADERS GET–TOGETHER

*TOMATO BOUILLON

*TUNA PIE WITH OAT BISCUIT CRUST

**PEACH AND COTTAGE CHEESE SALAD *See page 70*

**DATE NUT BARS *See page 103*

TOMATO BOUILLON

Combine 1 can (10½ oz.) condensed beef bouillon, 1 can (10¾ oz.) condensed tomato soup and 2 soup cans water. Bring to a boil. Serve hot in mugs, with minced parsley or chives as garnish. *Makes 6 servings.*

TUNA PIE WITH OAT BISCUIT CRUST

Filling:

½ teaspoon coarsely grated lemon peel

2 cans (6½ oz. or 7 oz. each) tuna, drained

1 can (10½ oz.) condensed cream of mushroom soup

⅓ cup light cream

2 hard-cooked eggs, quartered

3 tablespoons chopped pimiento

1 tablespoon minced fresh parsley

Crust:

¾ cup Aunt Jemima Pancake Mix

¼ Cup Quaker Oats (quick or old fashioned, uncooked)

3 tablespoons shortening

¼ cup milk

Add lemon peel to well-drained tuna, stir with fork to blend. Combine soup and cream; add to tuna with remaining filling ingredients. Pour into 1½ quart casserole.

For crust, combine pancake mix and oats; cut in shortening. Stir in milk until dry ingredients are moistened and dough can be formed into ball. Turn out on lightly floured board, roll ¼ inch thick into circle large enough to cover top of casserole. Cut a slash in center. Place over filling. Bake uncovered in oven preheated to 400° F., about 35 minutes, until golden. *Makes 4–6 servings.*

FOR A GOURMET GATHERING

AVOCADO-GRAPEFRUIT SALAD

*CREPES FLORENTINE

*MAPLE VELVET PIE

*COFFEE NEOPOLITAN

CREPES FLORENTINE

Crepes:

1 cup Aunt Jemima Buttermilk Pancake Mix

1¼ cups milk

2 eggs, beaten

Butter or margarine

Filling and Sauce:

1 can (10½ oz.) condensed cream of mushroom soup

½ cup light cream

1 teaspoon dry mustard

1 teaspoon Worcestershire sauce

1 package (10 oz.) frozen chopped spinach, thawed

1 cup diced cooked chicken or turkey

1 cup shredded Gruyere cheese

Crepes: Combine pancake mix, milk and eggs; beat until smooth. Melt a small amount of butter in small (6- or 7-inch) skillet; pour 1 tablespoon batter in skillet, tilt pan so batter covers bottom. When firm on bottom, flip crepe, cook on other side. Repeat until all batter is used.

Filling and Sauce: Combine soup, cream, mustard and Worcestershire; heat, stirring, until well-blended. Add spinach, chicken and half the cheese;

cook over low heat until cheese is melted. Place 1 tablespoon filling in each crepe; roll up, place overlapped side down in shallow casserole. When all crepes are filled, add remaining cheese to remaining sauce, spoon over filled crepes. Keep warm. Just before serving, place casserole under broiler until top is lightly glazed. *Makes 6 servings.*

MAPLE VELVET PIE

½ package (1 cup) Flako Pie Crust Mix, or pastry for 1-crust pie
1 envelope unflavored gelatine
¼ cup cold water
1 cup Aunt Jemima Syrup

3 eggs, separated
½ teaspoon salt
1 teaspoon vanilla
½ cup chopped pecans
1 cup heavy cream, whipped

Prepare baked 9-inch pie crust with pie crust mix according to package directions (or your favorite recipe).

Soften gelatine in cold water. Combine syrup, egg yolks and salt in saucepan. Cook over medium heat, stirring constantly until slightly thickened. Remove from heat; add softened gelatine, stir until dissolved. Add vanilla. Chill until partially set. Beat with rotary beater until fluffy and caramel-colored. Stir in pecans. Beat egg whites until stiff; fold into gelatine mixture. Fold in whipped cream. Mound into cooled pie shell, and chill until set. *Makes one 9-inch pie.*

COFFEE NEOPOLITAN

Prepare Espresso-type coffee; (use 1 cup Italian-roast coffee to 3 cups water). Then pour 1½ teaspoons cognac in each cup or heat-proof glass, and fill with hot coffee. Top with sweetened whipped cream and a sprinkle of cinnamon. Serve at once. *Makes 6 servings.*

SLUMBER PARTY MORNING AFTER

*AMBROSIA NECTAR

*CREAMED TURKEY OR TUNA ON WAFFLES

*APPLE CRISP *See page 60.*

MILK   COCOA

AMBROSIA NECTAR

1 banana, quartered
1 can (6 oz.) frozen orange juice concentrate, reconstituted

2 tablespoons shredded coconut

Combine banana, orange juice and shredded coconut in blender. Blend until smooth. *Makes 6 breakfast cocktails.*

CREAMED TURKEY ON WAFFLES

1½ cups diced cooked turkey
1 can (10½ oz.) condensed cream of mushroom soup
½ cup light cream or half-and-half

1 tablespoon minced parsley
1 package frozen Aunt Jemima Country Waffles

Combine turkey, soup and cream; cook, stirring, until heated through. Sprinkle with parsley just before serving. Prepare frozen waffles in toaster or oven according to package directions. Serve creamed turkey over hot waffles. *Makes 6 servings.*

Creamed Tuna on Waffles: Instead of turkey in above recipe, use 1 large can (13 oz.) chunk-style tuna, well-drained.

CHAPTER IV

Suppers and Simple Buffets

Sometimes it's a light and easy repast to serve before the theater or an evening of bridge. Again, the occasion calls for a touch of elegance—delicate stuffed crepes or a colorful pie with flaky, tender crust. Whether the dishes are homey and traditional, adapted foreign specialties, or quickly assembled casseroles made with mixes and pantry shelf supplies, a bit of imagination can make them memorable.

NEW NEIGHBOR WELCOME

FRENCH ONION SOUP

*VEGETABLE SALAD WHEEL

*VINAIGRETTE DRESSING

HOT CORN STICKS

*PROFITEROLES

VEGETABLE SALAD WHEEL

1 small head cauliflower	Lettuce
8 baby carrots, each quartered lengthwise	2 cups cooked whole green beans
1 package (10 oz.) frozen asparagus spears	Vinaigrette Dressing (see below)
1 package (10 oz.) frozen artichoke hearts	

Cook cauliflower, carrots, asparagus and artichoke hearts separately in salted water until just barely tender. Drain; chill. To serve, place cauliflower in center of round platter, surrounded with lettuce. Over lettuce, place remaining vegetables around the cauliflower like spokes in a wheel. Sprinkle half the Vinaigrette Dressing over vegetables; pass remainder in sauce boat. *Makes 8 servings.*

VINAIGRETTE DRESSING

½ cup oil	1 tablespoon chopped parsley
¼ cup vinegar	1 tablespoon capers
1 teaspoon salt	1 tablespoon chopped pimiento
¼ teaspoon pepper	
1 hard-cooked egg, chopped	

Combine all ingredients in glass jar; shake well. *Makes about ¾ cup.*

PROFITEROLES

1 package Flako Popover Mix	6 eggs
¾ cup butter or margarine	Vanilla ice cream
1½ cups water	Chocolate sauce

Preheat oven to 450° F. Lightly grease baking sheet. Place butter and water in 2-quart saucepan, bring to a boil over high heat until butter melts. Reduce heat, add popover mix, beat vigorously until mixture leaves sides of pan in compact ball. Remove from heat, add eggs one at a time, beating smooth after each addition; continue beating until mixture has satin sheen. Drop by rounded tablespoons on baking sheet, bake 20 minutes at 450° F., reduce temperature to 350° F., bake 30 minutes longer, or until golden. Cool. Cut in half horizontally. Just before serving, fill each with ice cream, replace top, serve lavished with chocolate sauce, allowing 2 or 3 to a serving. *Makes 6 servings.* *Note:* Remaining Profiteroles may be frozen for future use.

TEEN DATE

*PINK VICHYSSOISE

*HAM 'N CHEESE MONTE CARLO

**LEMON MERINGUE PIE *See page 106.*

PINK VICHYSSOISE

2 cans (10½ oz.) frozen condensed cream of potato soup	1 soup can light cream
	2 cups chilled tomato juice

Combine soup, cream and tomato juice, beat until smooth. Serve in chilled bowls with minced parsley or minced chives sprinkled over the top of each. *Makes 6 servings.*

HAM 'N CHEESE MONTE CARLO

¾ cup Aunt Jemima
  Buttermilk Pancake Mix
2 eggs
¾ cup milk
4 thin slices cooked
  ham

4 slices American cheese
8 slices white bread,
  crusts trimmed
Butter or margarine

Combine pancake mix, eggs and milk; beat until smooth. Make sandwiches of ham and cheese between slices of buttered bread; cut each in quarters. Dip sandwich quarters in the batter, holding at edge of bowl so that excess batter drips off. Sauté in butter until browned on each side. Serve 4 quarters (1 full sandwich) to each person. *Makes 4 servings.*

Ham 'N Cheese Fritters: Prepare exactly as for Ham 'N Cheese Monte Carlo, but instead of sautéeing, fry batter-dipped sandwich quarters in hot deep fat heated to 400° F. until crisp and brown on both sides. Drain on absorbent paper; serve warm.

EAST INDIAN SPREAD

*CURRIED LAMB

*GRITS RING

CHUTNEY

*CHAPATI

DICED ORANGES AND DATES

CURRIED LAMB

1½ lbs. lean lamb, cut
  into 1-inch cubes
2 tablespoons shortening
1 tablespoon curry powder
1 medium onion, minced
1 garlic clove, minced

1 apple, peeled and
  chopped
1½ cups beef bouillon
¼ cup cream

Sauté the lamb in shortening until well-browned on all sides; add curry powder, onion and garlic; cook until onion is soft. Add apple and bouillon. Simmer, covered, 1½ hours until meat is tender. Stir in cream and heat through. Serve in a Grits Ring (see below). *Makes 6 servings.*

GRITS RING

1¼ cups Quaker Enriched
  White Hominy Grits*

5 cups boiling water
1¼ teaspoons salt

Slowly stir grits into boiling salted water; cover and cook over low heat 25 to 30 minutes, stirring frequently. Pour into greased ring mold; let stand at room temperature about 25 minutes. Unmold on round platter; fill center with Curried Lamb. *Makes 6 servings.*

To use quick grits, increase grits to 1½ cups. Cook uncovered 2½ to 5 minutes, stirring occasionally.

CHAPATI

1¼ cups Aunt Jemima
  Pancake Mix

⅓ cup water

Place pancake mix in bowl, gradually add water, working it into the mix to form a soft dough. Divide into 8 pieces, flatten each into circles on a lightly floured board. Cover with towel, let stand 20 minutes. Roll out very thin on lightly floured board. Bake one at a time in an *ungreased* skillet or griddle, turning frequently until crisp and lightly browned, but avoid getting them too brown. Push down with a spatula as they cook to keep flat. Allow to cool slightly before serving so that they will become very crisp. *Makes 8 chapati,* to be served with curry in place of bread.

When It's a Party

Four ways to welcome company with "something different" menus tailored to please varied tastes. They're crowd-pleasers you can count on—hearty, wholesome, always popular.

DOWN EAST SUNDAY SUPPER

CLAM AND TOMATO JUICE

*CODFISH CAKES

*BOSTON BAKED BEANS

*COLE SLAW

*INDIAN PUDDING

CODFISH CAKES

2 packages (4 oz. each) shredded salt codfish	1 egg, beaten
1 to 1½ tablespoons instant minced onion	¼ teaspoon black pepper
2 cups hot, seasoned mashed potatoes	¼ cup (about) Quaker Enriched Corn Meal (yellow or white)
	6 tablespoons shortening

Freshen codfish according to package directions. Reconstitute onion in 2 tablespoons water. Mix codfish with mashed potatoes, egg, pepper and onion. Cool or chill until can be handled easily. Form into 3-inch cakes or patties. Roll cakes in corn meal. Brown on both sides in hot shortening. Serve with catsup on the side. *Makes 8–12 cakes.*

BOSTON BAKED BEANS

2 cans (1 lb. each) New England-style pork and beans	1 tablespoon catsup
½ cup Aunt Jemima Syrup	6 bacon slices, cooked and crumbled; or 6 frankfurters, cut in 1-inch pieces
1 teaspoon prepared mustard	
1 teaspoon instant minced onion	

Combine all ingredients, place in bean pot or 1½-quart baking dish with cover. Bake at 325° F. about 45 minutes or until piping hot. If preferred, uncover, bake 15 minutes longer, or until sauce is reduced and thickened. Serve from pot. *Makes 6 servings.*

COLE SLAW

Combine ½ cup of mayonnaise, ¼ cup dairy sour cream, 1 tablespoon sugar, ¼ teaspoon salt, ⅛ teaspoon celery salt, a dash of paprika. Set aside. Shred 3 cups cabbage in bowl, season with salt and pepper, add dressing, toss lightly. *Makes 6 servings.*

INDIAN PUDDING

4 cups milk	½ cup light molasses
½ cup Quaker Enriched Corn Meal (yellow or white)	½ teaspoon salt
1 tablespoon butter or margarine	½ teaspoon ginger

Scald 2½ cups of the milk in top of double boiler over hot water. Combine corn meal with ½ cup of the cold milk in saucepan, add hot milk, stirring constantly. Cook 25 minutes, stirring occasionally. Add butter, molasses, salt and ginger. Pour into buttered 1½-quart baking dish. Pour remaining 1 cup cold milk over top. Set baking dish in pan of water, bake covered in preheated slow oven (300° F.) about 2 hours. Uncover; continue baking 1 hour longer. Serve warm topped with cream or ice cream. *Makes 6 servings.*

ELEGANT BUT SIMPLE SUPPER

Pictured on page 47.

*LOBSTER CREPES MORNAY

*SPINACH SALAD MIMOSA

*HOT ROLLS

*CHOCO-PEPPERMINT ICE CREAM PIE

LOBSTER CREPES MORNAY

1 cup Mornay Sauce (page 27)	½ cup milk
1 can (about 5 oz.) lobster, drained and flaked	2 eggs
	Butter
½ cup Aunt Jemima Pancake Mix	2 tablespoons grated Swiss or Parmesan cheese

Reserve about ⅓ cup of Mornay Sauce for topping. Add lobster to remaining sauce. Place pancake mix, milk and eggs in bowl; beat until batter is fairly smooth. Put small amount of butter in small (7-inch) skillet; melt butter, than add *1 tablespoon* batter, tilting pan so bottom is covered evenly. Bake each crepe until delicately browned on each side. Add additional butter to skillet as needed before baking remaining crepes. Spread crepes while warm with lobster-sauce mixture; roll up. Place filled crepes, overlapping side down, in greased shallow casserole. Spread reserved sauce over top of filled crepes. Sprinkle cheese over sauce. Bake in oven preheated to 425° F. until cheese is melted and sauce is lightly glazed. *Makes 4–6 servings.*

HOT ROLLS

For 1 package refrigerator rolls, combine 1 tablespoon butter with 3 tablespoons sesame seed in small saucepan. Toast seed for a few minutes, brush on rolls, bake as directed.

SPINACH SALAD MIMOSA

1 lb. fresh spinach	3 hard-cooked eggs, minced or grated
6 slices bacon, cooked, crumbled	½ cup garlic-flavored French dressing

Soak spinach in cold water for 15 minutes. Lift from water; repeat. Break off stems, shake leaves well, tear into pieces, store in covered vegetable freshener until shortly before serving. Thoroughly chill bacon and eggs separately. At serving time, combine in salad bowl, toss with French dressing. *Makes 4–6 servings.*

CHOCO-PEPPERMINT ICE CREAM PIE

½ package (1 cup) Flako Pie Crust Mix, or pastry for 1-crust pie	1½ cups chocolate ice cream, softened
1½ cups peppermint ice cream, softened	Crushed peppermint candy

Prepare baked 9-inch pie crust with pie crust mix according to package directions (or your favorite recipe). Cool. Place the two kinds of ice cream in pie shell in layers or patches; with a spoon ripple through to make a marbleized or swirled pattern. Sprinkle candy over top. Place in freezer until time to serve. *Makes one 9-inch pie.*

Barbecue it! Kabob it! Midwest Sweet 'N Sour Ribs, recipe, p. 49; Picnic Kabobs and Dixie-style Skillet Corn Bread, p. 50. Great indoors or out!

Overleaf—An elegant yet simple buffet supper sure to please— Lobster Crepes Mornay, Spinach Salad Mimosa, and Choco-Peppermint Ice Cream Pie. Recipes, p. 44.